YET I WAIT

Brenda L. Jackson

Copyright ©2009 by Brenda L. Jackson
1st Edition, 2009

Unless otherwise stated, all Scriptures references are taken from the King James Version (KJV) of the Bible. Definitions are adapted from the Strong's Exhaustive Concordance of the Bible and Webster's New Collegiate Dictionary.

All Rights Reserved. This book is protected under the copyright laws of the United States of America. No part of this book may be reproduced or transmitted in any form or by any means, electronic or mechanical, including photocopying, recording, or by any information storage and retrieval system, without permission in writing from the author.

BJ Publishing Co.
6825 Flaxseed Lane
Charlotte, NC 28216
Email: brewilder@juno.com
Web Address: http://www.shekinahglory.min

International Standard Book Number (ISBN) 978-0-578-02519-3

Yet I Wait

Table of Contents

Chapter 1
What Does It Mean to Wait On The Lord? 3

Chapter 2
How Should We Wait? 25

Chapter 3
The Benefits of Waiting 37

Postlude
Waiting the Final Word 51

Chapter 1

What Does It Mean to Wait on the Lord?

There is a four letter word in the Bible and in Webster's dictionary that has literally made society virtually uneasy on different occasions. What word am I referring too? Glad you asked; that word is wait. When we look at the world around us this is the last thing people want to do. We live in a society where it seems like everybody wants instant gratification and nobody wants to wait. If it's cold outside, we don't want to wait for our cars to warm up. If that's not enough we don't want to wait in traffic, or wait in line at the shopping center and let's not talk about waiting in the dreaded doctor's office. Simply put no one wants to wait. We even have the microwave to help us to prepare instant cooked meals in seconds, because we don't want to turn the stove on and wait to cook a complete meal. Last but not least, we go through drive through lanes at McDonald's or Wendy's to get a quick meal.

I remember when Burger King use to have a slogan that went, "Have it Your Way" and today's society want just that, "their way", which equates to right now because I don't want to wait. Almost everything we do involve to some degree a type of waiting period, whether we are aware of it or not.

In this book I want to discuss what does it mean to wait on the Lord and what can happen while we are waiting on Him? With that said, let's answer the first question. In the Biblical sense waiting on God means to cease, stop and cut out all activities and put our mind on the Father. The word is further defined as to watch, observe, take heed, beware, cease, forbear, hold peace, quiet oneself, rest, seek, look for, hope, expect, linger for, and look eagerly for.

Did you know that there's another definition associated with waiting, and it is pain or grief? *Psalms 37:7 reads, "Rest in the LORD, and wait patiently for him:"* This word *wait* in this verse has several meanings. In the original Hebrew, it means to twist or whirl (in a circular or spiral manner), i.e. (specifically) to dance, to writhe in pain (especially of parturition-childbirth) or fear; figuratively, to wait, to pervert-to change or misapply the meaning of.

In the KJV it means bear, (make to) bring forth, (make to) calve (give birth to), dance, drive away, fall grievously (with pain), fear, form, great, grieve, (be) grievous, hope, look, make, be in pain, be much (sore) pained, rest, shake, shapen, (be) sorrow (- ful), stay, tarry, travail (with pain), tremble, trust, wait carefully (patiently), be wounded. Sounds like to me waiting is not always going to be something that we ease through, but we haven't been taught that.

Rest, that is to say, according to the meaning in the Hebrew text it means to be dumb; by implication, to be astonished, to stop; also to perish: which means being speechless due to sudden wonder or great surprise, amazement or fear; to stop means to cease, quit, and perish means to be destroyed, ultimately wiped out or die. The KJV definition is to cease, be cut down (off), forbear, hold peace, quietself, rest, be silent, keep (put to) silence, be (stand) still, tarry, wait. Resting and waiting seem to be similar in meanings and characteristics. I would assume that we can't have one without the other; look like they are twins.

As mentioned earlier to wait on the Lord in the Biblical sense means to cease, stop and cut out all activities and put our mind on the Father. This is when we begin to search for, seek for and inquire of the Lord; we are looking for directions or in search of answers. It doesn't mean we just sit down and do nothing while we wait. What it does mean is, while we are waiting, we continue praying, and reading, worshiping and all the things we would normally do while we wait to hear from Him concerning a matter. The searching, seeking and inquiring is all done because we want to hear what the Lord has to say.

That's why often times we will say I need a Word from the Lord. All we are saying is we are desirous of communication with God. In order to hear from Him we have to seek His face in the spirit. *Psalms 27:8 reads, "When thou saidst "Seek ye my face; my heart said unto thee, Thy face, LORD, will I seek"*. Why didn't the psalmist say my mouth said unto thee? I believe he said this because he knew according to *1 Sam 16:7, for the Lord seeth not as man seeth; for man looketh on the outward appearance, but the Lord looketh on the heart."* God looks at the heart and not at what comes out of our mouth? We can't seek the Lord with lip service it has to be from the heart. It's what's in our hearts that our mouth will speak. *Luke 6:45 reads, "A good man out of the good treasure of his heart bringeth forth that which is good; and an evil man out of the evil treasure of his heart bringeth forth that which is evil: for of the abundance of the heart his mouth speaketh"*. Whatever is in our heart will eventually come out our mouth.

In Christendom we are told when we can't seem to find direction or don't understand something to pray and "wait on the Lord". Often times someone will quote *Psalms 27:14, "Wait on the LORD: be of good courage, and he shall strengthen thine heart: wait, I say, on the LORD"*, or even *Proverbs 3:5-6 Trust in the Lord with all thine heart; and lean not unto thine own understanding. In all thy ways acknowledge him, and he shall direct thy paths"*. I don't know about you, but I've gotten it a lot and said it to people myself. These are wonderful exhortations and words of encouragement. However, how many of us know as we just found out to wait on the Lord can be grievous at times. You would think that it wouldn't be because we have all this Word to keep us in perfect peace. Why then can it be grievous or even hard? I'll tell you why because we as fallen humanity are so prone to take matters into our own hands. We figure we can solve our problems on our own without waiting on the Father.

The thing about all of this is a lot of times no one tells us that waiting can be hard and grievous. Nor do they tell us what we can expect to experience while we are waiting. Nobody talks about all the ugly stuff and what happens when you're not in perfect peace before the breakthrough comes. I want to talk about some of the ugly stuff…Can we talk about that? See anybody can say you need to wait, or tell you why you have to wait and what the fruits are of your waiting. Nevertheless, what will one experience? If you are like me you need to know what you are going to have to face. Let's just think about the ugly stuff for a minute. What about the times we got mad with God or when we really didn't want to hear what He had to say so we tuned the Holy Spirit out. Or what about when we didn't like the answer we got. What about when it seemed like God was taking to long to answer so we took matters in our own hand. How about when you didn't want to hear another quoted Scripture? We've all been there at one time or the other. If you haven't; then keep living you will have your moment. Notify your face that it is not a pretty picture. I know from experience that waiting can be one of the most frustrating and aggravating times in a person's life. Maybe you've been there, and you made out like a champ, but there was a time I didn't. If you would be truthful neither did you.

During my time of waiting my flesh was a terrible mess. No matter how many scriptures I quoted my flesh was not trying to hear it. Why? Because the bottom line is my flesh doesn't want to submit. My flesh wants to take matters in its own hand. Anybody been there besides me? Until I caused my flesh to obey, I was a wreck. Paul put it this way in, *1 Cor. 9:27, "But I keep under my body, and bring it into subjection."*

Notice Paul said I keep under my body that means to subdue to cause it to comply, and he didn't say God did it. One of the major problems with the saints is we think God is suppose to do everything. Paul knows he's responsible for his flesh and the mess it can cause. As a result, he goes on to say and bring it into subjection. Subjection means to enslave, bring under authority or control. Enslave how? Enslave it to the Word of God. Our flesh has to comply (to act in accordance with a request, rule or order) and become a slave to the Word. Enslaving our body to the Word keeps it under and brings it into subjection. We have to make it obey; we must make our flesh act according to the Word of God.

What's happening is our flesh is having a fit while our spirit man is calm by reason of the Word. Our spirit is saying more of the Word and our flesh is saying act like a fool. Our flesh doesn't want to be calm and definitely does not want to obey the Word. Paul put it this way in *Gal 5:17, "For the flesh lusteth against the Spirit, and the Spirit against the flesh: and these are contrary the one to the other: so that ye cannot do the things that ye would"*.

I learned a long time ago that I had better talk to my flesh and tell it what to do, or else it will talk to me, and I'd find myself doing exactly what it wants. We have to continue to feed our spirit the Word and at the same time make our flesh obey the Word. There is a struggle in our flesh that will always say forget it all, I've had enough, but the Spirit of God chimes through all the mess to say "Wait I Say On the Lord."

Earlier I stated I became frustrated and aggravated. Well, those aren't the only things that happened while

I was waiting. I got anxious, impatient, angry, and fearful. Anybody ever got mad with God and blamed Him. Let's be truthful about the matter we probably could think of more than these.

For example, there was a time when I had to wait on the Lord because I had been laid off work. I was on severance pay for one year, but around the end of the tenth month I got myself so worked up (I panicked) until I started walking up and down my hallway practically screaming because I couldn't get a response from God right away. I experienced a lot of anxiety, frustration, fear; and impatience during this time. I was questioning God, why me Lord? When are you going to answer? Lord I need a job, I got bills! You said you would answer me in a time a trouble! I went through the whole nine yards of not knowing how to wait on God. I was a mess.

Again I say it wasn't pretty. Trust me; I wasn't trying to quote scriptures or anything like that. When we are in the flesh there really isn't anything we can do or God will do until we settle ourselves. Why? The base or soulish part of our nature is in operation; Paul said in, *Rom. 8:8 "So then they that are in the flesh cannot please God."* Everything I mentioned has to do with our soulish realm where our emotions are housed, which has nothing to do with our Spirit. It is all flesh. We will never get anywhere with God in the flesh. It was only after I calmed down and got before the Lord in prayer and read the Word did I get an answer.

The end of the matter is I received an email the same day I had my temper tantrum from the company where I had been laid off. They were requesting that I complete the necessary hiring documents. Mind you I hadn't interviewed with the hiring manager or anything like that. I said to myself this is not the way people are hired with this company. Usually a person is interviewed by the hiring manager, the job offer is made and then all the necessary paperwork is completed. Everything was done opposite of the way it's normally done. Then the Holy Spirit reminded me that God ways are not like our ways. I begin to thank the Lord and tell Him I know this is You because no one else could do this but You. I also had to ask forgiveness for acting the way I did.

Needless to say the interviewed was arranged, all the documentation completed and the job offer was made. I want you to know that God worked it out so that when I went back to work there wasn't an interruption in my paycheck, all my previous years of service were reinstated, I got four weeks of vacation, my job title and salary remained the same. It was just as if I had never been laid off. I guess you could say I had been on a ten month paid vacation.

Even though I panicked I sought the Lord. *Ps 34:4 states, "I sought the LORD, and he heard me, and delivered me from all my fears."* We have no need to fear. This verse lets us know that when we seek, inquire, ask of the Lord, He will hear, and he will deliver us from all our fears. Not one fear but all fears. He doesn't stop at one He wants us free from all. Fear is an emotion. We've got to get to a point in our lives where we really get our emotions under control and not let them control us.

In *Psalms 130:5 it reads, "I wait for the LORD, my soul doth wait, and in his word do I hope. My soul waiteth for the Lord more than they that watch for the morning: I say, more than they that watch for the morning."* David says he waits for the Lord. Sounds like David got his soul (flesh), his emotions, and his will to wait. He goes on to say that it's gotten to the point that his soul, his emotions, and his will waits for the Lord more than they that watch for the morning. We've heard people say I can't wait until the morning, or I can't wait until tomorrow, but David said my soul is waiting more than that for the Lord; not only that, his hope is in God's Word. Whatever God has to say that will be his hope or his trust. I believe if David was here today he'd say like some of us, Lord if I could just hear one word.

Let's look at some Scriptures that show that we aren't the only ones who have had some issues with waiting. These scriptures will help us to see what others experienced and what they did.

Genesis 15:1-7

15:1 After these things the word of the LORD came unto Abram in a vision, saying, Fear not, Abram: I am thy shield, and thy exceeding great reward.
15:2 And Abram said, Lord GOD, what wilt thou give me, seeing I go childless, and the steward of my house is this Eliezer of Damascus?
15:3 And Abram said, Behold, to me thou hast given no seed: and, lo, one born in my house is mine heir.
15:4 And, behold, the word of the LORD came unto him, saying, This shall not be thine heir; but he that shall come forth out of thine own bowels shall be thine heir.
15:5 And he brought him forth abroad, and said, Look now toward heaven, and tell the stars, if thou be able to number them: and he said unto him, So shall thy seed be.
15:6 And he believed in the LORD; and he counted it to him for righteousness.

Genesis 16: 1-6

16:1 Now Sarai Abram's wife bare him no children: and she had an handmaid, an Egyptian, whose name was Hagar.

16:2 And Sarai said unto Abram, Behold now, the LORD hath restrained me from bearing: I pray thee, go in unto my maid; it may be that I may obtain children by her. And Abram hearkened to the voice of Sarai.
16:3 And Sarai Abram's wife took Hagar her maid the Egyptian, after Abram had dwelt ten years in the land of Canaan, and gave her to her husband Abram to be his wife.
16:4 And he went in unto Hagar, and she conceived: and when she saw that she had conceived, her mistress was despised in her eyes.
16:5 And Sarai said unto Abram, My wrong be upon thee: I have given my maid into thy bosom; and when she saw that she had conceived, I was despised in her eyes: the LORD judge between me and thee.
16:6 But Abram said unto Sarai, Behold, thy maid is in thy hand; do to her as it pleaseth thee *. And when Sarai dealt hardly with her, she fled from her face.

It's apparent in the beginning of this scripture that Abram wants a child, an heir to him. Therefore the Lord assures him that he will have a child that will come from his own loins. According to scripture, Abraham believed what God said.
15:2 And Abram said, Lord GOD, what wilt thou give me, seeing I go childless, and
the steward of my house is this Eliezer of Damascus?

15:4 And, behold, the word of the LORD came unto him, saying, This shall not be thine heir; but he that shall come forth out of thine own bowels shall be thine heir
15:6 And he believed in the LORD; and he counted it to him for righteousness.

Scripture lets us know that Sarai came up with a plan to have a child, so she told Abram her thoughts, and he went along with it. This passage reads Abraham hearkened to the voice of Sarai. *Hearkened* means to hear, listen to, obey and to hear with attention or interest.
16:2 And Sarai said unto Abram, Behold now, the LORD hath restrained me from bearing: I pray thee, go in unto my maid; it may be that I may obtain children by her. And Abram hearkened to the voice of Sarai.

As a result of this plan devised by Sarah and Abram consenting to it, this is what happened while they were waiting on the promise of God:
1. **Abraham is anxious to have an heir.** *15:2 And Abram said, Lord GOD, what wilt thou give me, seeing I go childless, and the steward of my house is this Eliezer of Damascus?*
   15:3 And Abram said, Behold, to me thou hast given no seed: and, lo, one born in my house is mine heir.

Phil. 4:6 reads, Be careful for nothing; but in every thing by prayer and supplication with thanksgiving let your requests be made known unto God.

2. **Sarah gives Hagar to Abraham** and he doesn't say no or remind Sarah of the promise. **Hagar despised Sarah** when she finds out she's pregnant.
   16:4 And he went in unto Hagar, and she conceived: and when she saw that she had conceived, her mistress was despised in her eyes.

3. **Sarah dealt hardly with Hagar** in other words she mistreated Hagar.
   16:6 Abram said unto Sarai, Behold, thy maid is in thy hand; do to her as it pleaseth thee *. And when Sarai dealt hardly with her, she fled from her face.

4. **There's conflict between Isaac and Ishmael** right after Isaac is weaned. Jealousy and resentment is the end results of all this.
   21:9 And Sarah saw the son of Hagar the Egyptian, which she had born unto Abraham, mocking.

5. **Sarah blames Abraham for what has happened**
   16:5 And Sarai said unto Abram, My wrong be upon thee: I have given my maid into thy bosom;

and when she saw that she had conceived, I was despised in her eyes: the LORD judge between me and thee.
16:6 But Abram said unto Sarai, Behold, thy maid is in thy hand; do to her as it pleaseth thee *. And when Sarai dealt hardly with her, she fled from her face.

6. **Sarah wants Hagar and her child sent away.** She doesn't want Isaac and Ishmael to grow up together.
   21:10 Wherefore she said unto Abraham, Cast out this bondwoman and her son for the son of this bondwoman shall not be heir with my son, even with Isaac.

7. **Abraham was grieved** because of his son and God said do what Sarah wants.
   21:11 And the thing was very grievous in Abraham's sight because of his son
   21:12 And God said unto Abraham, Let it not be grievous in thy sight because of the lad, and because of thy bondwoman; in all that Sarah hath said unto thee, hearken unto her voice; for in Isaac shall thy seed be called.

This is why things are so intense in the Middle East it's all about Abraham's children Isaac and Ishmael. When Abraham gave Hagar water and food and sent

Ishmael and her away that was the beginning of what would continue up to this day. Ishmael became the great leader of the Arabs (most of whom are Muslims) and they claim, because Ishmael was the firstborn of Abram, the Promised Land is theirs. The Jews which is Isaac's seed believe that the Promised Land is theirs, as God's covenant was not with Ishmael but with Isaac.

This jealousy and resentment have created hate between these two nations for many years. It's about the deed to the land of Israel which God promised to Abraham seed, which is Isaac. It's not about oil or their government. *Gal 4:28-30 reads, "Now we, brethren, as Isaac was, are the children of promise. But as then he that was born after the flesh persecuted him that was born after the Spirit, even so it is now. Nevertheless what saith the scripture? Cast out the bondwoman and her son: for the son of the bondwoman shall not be heir with the son of the freewoman."* Ishmael had been "born according to the flesh" while Isaac had been "born according to the promise". Isaac replaced Ishmael as the favored son and heir. This, of course, made Ishmael jealous and bitter. As a result, he mocked his half-brother.

Please get this when we don't wait on the Lord everything that follows has to do with our flesh and not the spirit. All of what happened to Abraham and

Sarah could have been avoided if they had waited. That's why it is so important to walk in the Spirit at all times. Paul put it this way in *Galatians 5:16, "This I say then, Walk in the Spirit, and ye shall not fulfil the lust of the flesh."* Sarah and Abraham made provision for the flesh and this was the end results. When we don't fulfill the lust or desires of our flesh then we can understand what these two scriptures mean. *Romans 8:1,4 "There is therefore now no condemnation to them which are in Christ Jesus, who walk not after the flesh, but after the Spirit.* Verse 4, *"That the righteousness of the law might be fulfilled in us, who walk not after the flesh, but after the Spirit."*

There is yet another time when a person was told by God to wait and didn't. Let's look at 1 Samuel 10:1-9. These verses focus on the time when Samuel privately anointed Saul as king. Samuel told Saul in the previous chapter to tell his servant to ahead of them because he had to give him a word from God.

10:1 Then Samuel took a vial of oil, and poured it upon his head, and kissed him, and said, Is it not because the Lord hath anointed thee to be captain over his inheritance?
2 When thou art departed from me to day, then thou shalt find two men by Rachel's sepulchre in the border of Benjamin at Zelzah; and they will say unto thee, The asses which thou wentest to seek are found: and,

lo, thy father hath left the care of the asses, and sorroweth for you, saying, What shall I do for my son?
3 Then shalt thou go on forward from thence, and thou shalt come to the plain of Tabor, and there shall meet thee three men going up to God to Bethel, one carrying three kids, and another carrying three loaves of bread, and another carrying a bottle of wine:
4 And they will salute thee, and give thee two loaves of bread; which thou shalt receive of their hands.
5 After that thou shalt come to the hill of God, where is the garrison of the Philistines: and it shall come to pass, when thou art come thither to the city, that thou shalt meet a company of prophets coming down from the high place with a psaltery, and a tabret, and a pipe, and a harp, before them; and they shall prophesy:
6 And the Spirit of the Lord will come upon thee, and thou shalt prophesy with them, and shalt be turned into another man.
7 And let it be, when these signs are come unto thee, that thou do as occasion serve thee; for God is with thee.
8 And thou shalt go down before me to Gilgal; and, behold, I will come down unto thee, to offer burnt offerings, and to sacrifice sacrifices of peace offerings: seven days shalt thou tarry, till I come to thee, and shew thee what thou shalt do.

9 And it was so, that when he had turned his back to go from Samuel, God gave him another heart: and all those signs came to pass that day.

Saul received the word from the prophet and started on his way and all the signs Samuel had spoken came to pass on that day. Notice Saul didn't have a problem in this area because all this happened the same day as Samuel said it would. However, it was only after the people officially made him king in Gilgal did his problem start. *1 Sam 11:15, "And all the people went to Gilgal; and there they made Saul king before the Lord in Gilgal; and there they sacrificed sacrifices of peace offerings before the Lord; and there Saul and all the men of Israel rejoiced greatly."*

One of the last things Samuel told Saul to do was to go to Gilgal. *1 Sam. 11:8 "And thou shalt go down before me to Gilgal; and, behold, I will come down unto thee, to offer burnt offerings, and to sacrifice sacrifices of peace offerings: seven days shalt thou tarry, till I come to thee, and shew thee what thou shalt do".*

Jonathan attacked the Philistines in Geba this caused the Philistines to come in numbers against Israel. When the men of Israel saw this they were distressed and begin to hide themselves in caves and other places. Some of the people followed Saul but they were afraid. Because Saul saw all that had taken place he panicked. He took it upon himself to offer a sacrifice, knowing that he wasn't a priest. He was given a command to wait seven days in Gilgal so that Samuel could offer the burnt offering, and to sacrifice sacrifices of peace offerings. *1 Samuel 13: 8 reads, "And he tarried seven days according to the set time that Samuel had appointed; the people were scattered from him."*

When Samuel didn't come as Saul expected he took it upon himself to offer the burnt offerings himself. How many of us have found ourselves in a similar situation? Moreover, because things weren't turning out the way we expected we became impatient and took matters into our own hands like Saul. Saul didn't have the authority to offer any offerings because he was not a Levite (a priest). He was from the tribe of Benjamin. Probably because he was king, he thought he could do whatever he wanted. We are like that at times and say things like: I got this or I'm in charge of this and wind up making matters worse. Like Saul we are guilty of choosing our own path. It's during these times we get ahead of God and make a mess of things. (This same kind of presumption cost king Uzziah and he paid for it dearly; see 2 Chron. 26:16-19.)

If Saul had waited for Samuel he was going to show him what to do; possibly, against the Philistines. He couldn't wait so he did his own thing. Saul emotions took over and he allowed his flesh to take charge of the situation, and as a result he ends up in complete disobedience. When Samuel arrived and found that Saul had offered a burnt offering, he rebuked him.) Saul gave excuses for why he didn't obey, such as: *(See 1 Samuel 13: 10-13*

- ***I saw the people were scattered from me*** – a form a fear and at the same time trying to gain the people's confidence.
- ***Thou camest not within the days appointed*** – you didn't come on time – impatience, blaming
- ***The Philistines gathered themselves together at Michmash*** - fear
- ***I forced myself therefore and offered a burnt offering.*** – He went against everything that he knew was right to do and **made himself do wrong. Never make yourself do wrong no matter what.**

As a result the kingship was taken from Him. How many know that there is no excuse, valid or invalid that will work when God gives a command to do something. When God says wait we need to wait. We can be like Saul at times when we become impatient and fearful, thereby proceeding to take matters into our own hands. Instead of doing what we know is right we do the wrong thing.

If nothing else we need to know that there are consequences when we don't wait. This can be seen in what happened with Abraham and Sarah. They had to live with the fact that Hagar's child would always be a rival to Isaac. Then there's Saul who lost the kingship because of disobedience. We all can learn a thing or two from these people so that we don't make similar mistakes.

Let me reiterate waiting means to stop all activities and focus on God. It means to rest in the Lord and wait expectantly, and to look eagerly for Him to respond to our prayers. While we are waiting, we need to walk in the Spirit and deny our flesh. Our flesh, which is our soulish nature which is our will, emotions and our intellect will cause us to take matters into our own hands, which will ultimately result in disobedience. In everything obey God. Again, I say wait on the Lord.

Chapter 2

How Should We Wait?

As mentioned in the previous chapter no one likes waiting and we as a society we want things right now. By definition the word itself makes the most of us cringe at the thought of having to do so. However, we have learned thus far that right now is not always the case when it comes to God. There will always be occasions where He will tell us to wait and make us wait. From the previous chapter, we've discovered what the Bible means when it says to wait. Now let us look at how we should wait, and as I share these practical principles let's embrace them and incorporate them into our daily living.

There are several scriptures which tell us how we should wait. Let's look at few and read what the writer had to say about the subject.

1. **Wait while praying** – *Psalms 25:4-5 - Shew me thy ways, O LORD; teach me thy paths. Lead me in thy truth, and teach me: for thou art the God of my salvation; on thee do I wait all the day.*

When we are waiting on God more than anything we need to be in prayer. We need to really pray, stop thinking, planning and talking to other folks. Why, because we need God to show and teach us his ways. It's good to hear how other people dealt with things, but sometimes we don't need to hear about what they did. We tend to try what someone else did thinking it will work for us. A lot times what God gave someone else is not for us it's for them. Don't be a copycat! We should stop mimicking others. We need to get before the Father and find out what He wants us to do. We need His guidance into His truth. This is the main purpose of waiting, simple put; we don't have a clue as to what we need to do, so we need Him to tell us. True, we need the counsel of others but only as a confirmation to what the Father has already revealed to us.

Shew in this verse means cause to know, learn to know or make known. In this prayer David is saying cause me to know your ways, direction, manner, or habit. In other words he's saying, Lord I want to know your way; I want to know your direction. I want to know how you would have me do things and the way I should go. Cause me to go in your truth or in your true doctrine of what you have already established.

The word *truth* in this verse can mean reliability and stability. Do you know God's word is reliable and you can stand on it? David goes on to say for you are the God of my salvation or my deliverance, rescue, safety, welfare, victory or prosperity. Because God is all this, David said I'll wait on you all day. People can be a lot of things to us but only the Father can be everything we need. Besides that God is a jealous God and that place which is only reserved for Him, he will not share with another.

2. **Look for God to move** – *Psalms 62:5-6 - My soul wait thou only upon God; for my expectation is from him. He only is my rock and my salvation: he is my defence: I shall not be moved.*

If we are to ever receive anything from the Father we have got to cause or make our soul, which is our mind, emotions, and our will to wait. We do this with expectation, meaning God has to become the object of our hope or confidence. Therefore, we wait. David said in this verse I expectantly wait on you God because you only are my rock. Rock is representative of strength, and we know a rock will not give way easily. Since the Rock is our strength, we can lean on it and never worry about it crumbling. Jesus is our Rock.

Our focus has to be on God alone. David goes on to say, He only is "my salvation". This is the same word David used earlier in *Psalms 25:5* and it has the same meaning. Once again there is an expectation for deliverance, rescue, safety, welfare, victory and prosperity. Look like to me salvation is tied to many things and with those just mentioned it covers all the basic needs we have in this life. We've must get to a point where we know that God is our only strength and deliverance. Everything hinges upon Him alone.

3. **Have a strong persistent desire** – *Psalms 130: 5-6 I wait for the LORD, my soul doth wait, and in his word do I hope. My soul waiteth for the Lord more than they that watch for the morning: I say, more than they that watch for the morning.*

We should have a strong persistent yearning or desire for the Lord. From this passage we can get an idea of the passion David had for the Lord. There are three things going on here.
    a) David said I wait for the Lord.
    b) He says my soul wait.
    c) Then he says, in his word do I hope

Waiting obviously requires discipline, because David said I wait for the Lord. I mentioned this in the previous chapter when we talked about what it means to wait. If there's no discipline we will go our own way and we all know to well what the consequences are of this. As a result, this should be a lesson for us; we've got to learn how to discipline ourselves to wait. Not only did he wait he got his soul to wait.

David was saying Lord I trust your word. I rely on or

trust in your Word. As we wait on and seek the Lord, it is always good to be mindful of the written Word of God, and what He's revealed in the past. The Word of God will sustain us while we wait. David goes on to say that it's gotten to the point that his soul waits for the Lord more than they that watch for the morning. I'm sure someone who works night shift could relate to watching for the morning. Even so, David said my soul waits more than they. Not only did he say it, he repeated it because He wants us to know just how much he is longing for God. Question is does God know how much we are longing for Him. Is it more than the morning?

4. **Focus only on God** – *Psalms 62:5 - My soul, wait thou only upon God; for my expectation is from Him.*

In order to wait on God, we've got to get our mind off everything else and let our focus only be on God. This involves an expectation of something special. Waiting means anticipation, and a confident hope in something that will take place. Whatever we are expecting is only going to come from God, he's the source. *Jeremiah 14:22* put it this way, *"Are there any among the vanities of the Gentiles that can cause raise? Or can the heavens give shower? Art thou he, O LORD our God? Therefore we will wait upon thee: for thou hast made all these things.*

We must learn to have a single and consistent focus on God as the source of life, because of who He is, and what He can and is able to do. *Ephesians 3:20* reads, *"Now unto Him who is able to do exceeding abundantly above all that we ask or think, according to the power that worketh in us"*. This verse simply put means God can go above and beyond what we ask Him, or what we think about.

5. **Let who we are display the character and nature of God** - *Psalms 25:21 Let integrity and uprightness preserve me; for I wait on thee.*

We are to let integrity and uprightness preserve us while we wait. *Integrity* means:
- Steadfast adherence to a strict moral or ethical code.
- The state of being unimpaired; soundness.
- The quality or condition of being whole or undivided; completeness

Integrity involves character attributes that determine a person's moral and ethical actions and reactions as well as an undivided or unbroken completeness or totality with nothing wanting. Our integrity and uprightness shows who we are, and what we are made of. The character and nature of God should always be on display in our lives. The word preserves means to be blockaded, to guard, to watch over and to keep. We should be totally stable and unwavering in our convictions, confessions and professions when it comes to the things of God.

James 1:8 reads, "A double minded man is unstable in all his ways." There shouldn't be anything divided or incomplete about our moral or ethical values. We should be the walking epistles that everyone can read. People ought to have good things to say about us. They should find us blameless and not acting like the world and all that is around us. *Philippians 2:15 reads, "That ye may be blameless and harmless, the sons of God, without rebuke, in the midst of a crooked and perverse nation, among whom ye shine as lights in the world;* We all should purpose to live like Daniel so that there is no error or fault found in us. *Dan 6:4 Then the presidents and princes sought to find occasion against Daniel concerning the kingdom; but they could find none occasion nor fault; forasmuch as he was faithful, neither was there any error or fault found in him.*

6. **Trust in God at all times** - *1 Peter 5:6 —Humble yourselves therefore yourselves therefore under the mighty hand of God, that he may exalt you in due time:*

Put aside all pride and our own agenda and demand humility. Reject what we know how to do and reject any thing that is without God. If we don't know what God wants us to do then we ought to do nothing. Wait on Him until we know what to do. Never walk in foolish ignorance of the Father's will. *Ephesians 5:17 reads "Wherefore be ye not unwise, but understanding what the will of the Lord is".*

Jesus didn't do anything on his own, so what makes us think we can. Jesus said in *John 5:30, "I can of mine own self do nothing: as I hear, I judge: and my judgment is just; because I seek not mine own will, but the will of the Father which hath sent me.*
Psalms 62:8 Trust in him at all times: ye people, pour out your heart before him: God is a refuge for us.
We are to trust in him at all times; no matter what the situation is. Not only are we to trust Him, we are to pour out our hearts before him.

There are times when we can't always find the words, but the Spirit knows. *Romans 8:26 reads, "Likewise the Spirit also helpeth our infirmities: for we know not what we should pray for as we ought: but the Spirit itself maketh intercession for us with groanings which cannot be uttered.* When we can't get it out the way we want to the Holy Spirit knows what we are saying, and He takes over and says what we can't. We can trust in the Lord He will keep our deepest secrets.

7. **Be patient** –*Psalms 37:7 Rest in the LORD, and wait patiently for him:*

Rest in this verse means to be or grow dumb, be silent, still, motionless or stand still. There will come a time while we are waiting on the Lord that we will be dumb. Why, because we really don't know what to do. We probably never thought of it as being dumb but what else can it be when we don't have any answers and we don't know what say.

Wait means to cease, hold peace, quiet self, be silent, be still, tarry, keep silence, but it also means pain, painful, grievous. We have learned that waiting can be painful and grievous at times. It is not a pretty picture. We are creatures of habit. We have a designated time when we think things ought to happen, so being patient is not an option for us. When things don't happen in our timeframe, we generally will take matters into our own hands. That's why *Psalms145:15* was written and it reads, *"Rest and wait patiently, do not fret."* To wait on the Lord means to rest and wait on His timing.

Let's take a few minutes to discuss time, because resting, waiting and being patient requires time. There are two ancient Greeks words for time, *chronos* and *kairos*. *Chronos* refers to chronological or sequential time. Chronos time is measured by the clock and calendar. It is orderly; it has a rhythm, and is predictable. It is what we typically think of as time. *Kairos* is a time, not measured by the clock or calendar, where God has chosen "the right moment" or the "opportune" time. Kairos time usually involves a period of disruption to the normal flow of things. Kairos is the "fullness of time," God's time zone. This is the time we want to shed a little light on. God created time, and in his sovereign kairos time, He interacts and enters into our chronos time according to His perfect will. That's why He can disrupt our little program and agenda at any given moment. He doesn't operate on our time (chronos). When we are waiting, it will be the right moment and the opportune time that He gives us what we've been expecting.

Let's look at two examples of kairos time, God's time. *Luke 19:41-44 "41 And when he was come near, he beheld the city, and wept over it, 42 Saying, If thou hadst known, even you, at least in this thy day, the things which belong unto thy peace! But now they are hid from thine eyes. 43 For the days shall come upon thee, that thine enemies shall cast a trench about thee, and compass thee round, and keep thee in on every side. 44 And shall lay thee even with the ground, and they children within thee; and they shall not leave in one stone upon another, because thou knowest not the time (kairos) of thy visitation.*

These verses show us how Jesus wept over Jerusalem because they missed their *kairos* time with God. They missed the day/time of their visitation. Surely God grieves over us when we miss our kairos moments with Him. *Romans 13:11 – And that, knowing the time, that now it is high time to awake out of sleep: for now is our salvation nearer than when we believed.* If we as the body of Christ don't wake up and perceive the time, we will miss our kairos moment/season with God. In chronos time, there is time to make decisions and God will usually wait for us to be obedient, but in kairos time, a kairos moment says, "Now is the time!" If the time/moment is missed, there is no getting it back. We need to make sure that while we rest and wait patiently that we don't miss God by getting caught up in our own time.

8. **Do things God's way** - *Psalms 37:34 Wait on the LORD, and keep his way...*

Why is keeping His way important? If nothing else comes to mind then it should be because it is commanded. The only other options we have is to do what's right in our own eyes, to take matters in our own hands and work our own agenda. How many know that our way is generally not God's way. If God has not clearly given the way we should take and if it's not according to His word and His infinite wisdom, then it is self-will. Self-will is sin. What we need to do is to seek his face and make sure our heart is ready to obey once He's made known to us His way. Just as the Son did nothing in and of himself so it should be with us. Bottom line, again I say if we don't know what His way is then don't do anything. Wait on Him. Keeping His way requires unquestionable obedience.

9. **Hope and quietly wait** – *Lamentations 3:26 It is good that a man should both hope and quietly wait for the salvation of the LORD.*

The writer said it's good that a man should have both hope and quietly wait for the salvation of the Lord. In other words our attitude should be to both hope and quietly wait for the deliverance of the Lord. This means no temper tantrums and no ungodly actions. We are to be still and know that God will deliver.

10. **Let this be our daily regiment** – Hosea 12:6 *Therefore turn thou to thy God; keep mercy and judgment, and wait on thy God continually.*

While we are waiting on the Lord we should turn to Him in everything and while doing so we are to be merciful and do the right thing. This is to be our daily routine. Job said, *"All the days of my appointed time will I wait, till my change come"*. *Job 14:14*

Chapter 3

The Benefits of Waiting

It's already been established that to wait on the Lord means to rest and wait on His timing. We've also found that resting, waiting and being patient requires time. In the previous chapter we talked about two ancient Greeks words for time, chronos and kairos. Let's review them once again. Chronos refers to chronological or sequential time. Chronos time is measured by the clock and calendar. When we are waiting it will be the right moment and the opportune time that He gives us what we've been expecting. Not only will He give us what we've been expecting, but also give us some extra. *Ephesians 3:20 reads, "Now unto him that is able to do exceeding abundantly above all that we ask or think, according to the power that worketh in us."* No matter what we've been waiting on or asking for He's able to supersede that.

The Father is able to go above and beyond what we've been waiting on and give us what we don't ask for. Ask Solomon, he asked for wisdom and knowledge God gave it to him. Not only did God give those things but gave riches, wealth and honor like no man before or after him. Look at all the extra he got without asking. God with His good self sees past our faults and see our needs. Isn't God the same today as He was in the days of old? I don't know about you but I can use the extra. With all the ugly stuff we have to endure while we wait nobody could have ever told me that there were extra benefits that come with the waiting.

Believe it or not there are several benefits we can receive by waiting on the Father. I'd like to call them benefits because these are things that happen behind the scene while we were sometimes cutting up or acting out. Let me throw this out there just in case someone might be thinking there's a shortcut to the benefits. If anybody is thinking that now is the time to notify your face that it's not so. At the end of the day, the only way we are going to reap the extra or anything from the Father is; when we buckle down, quiet ourselves and obey the voice of the Lord. There is no shortcut.

I think this is worth repeating. The only way we are going to reap the extra is when we buckle down, quiet ourselves and obey the voice of the Lord. We only get the benefits after obedience. All of these are prerequisites they are requirements we have to meet before the Father moves on our behalf. After all has been said and done we will see the results of our waiting. That's something to shout about because there is some good coming out of all this! Hallelujah!

Here are a few things we can look forward to at the end of the wait that I'm sure the Father will give us. Let's start with:

1. **Our prayers are answered** – *Psalm 40:1-3 says, "I waited patiently for the Lord; and He inclined unto me, and heard my cry. He brought me up also out of an horrible pit, out the miry clay and set my feet upon a rock and established my goings. And he hath put a new song in my mouth, even praises unto our God: many shall see it, and fear, and shall trust in the LORD"*

Usually before Father answers our prayers for provision, guidance or healing, He will require us to go through a season of waiting. For those of us who are unwilling to wait on God, we may fall into sin by trying to meet our needs ourselves or just missing His timing. In this passage of Scripture, it's possible that David was in despair or depressed based on the content of the other verses. Whatever he was experiencing, he talks about how he waited and when he waited it was done patiently. Meaning he didn't get frustrated or riled up and try to take matters in his own hands. He wasn't moaning, groaning, whining or complaining like we tend to do while waiting. He waited patiently. *Patiently*, in this sentence means he was expecting or looking for God to show up. Are you waiting on God to show up?

Sure enough through David's patience paid off. David penned, *"He inclined unto me". Inclined* means listens with interest, yield to, bend down to or turn aside to. God listened with interest; He turned aside or bent down to David. This shows how concerned the Father is about us. Whatever concerns us concerns the Father. Know that He is interested in you. *1 Peter 5:7* reads, *"Casting all your care upon him; for he careth for you."*

When God did this, He put himself in a position to hear David's cry. *Cry* here means cry for help. Looks like to me when we are in the right position, that is patiently waiting on him then God can position himself to help us. Scripture goes on to say not only did he hear David's cry, but He saw where David was and did something about it. There are five things that God did for David. Let's take a look at them and see how they might apply to us.

Brought me up also out of an horrible pit – Sometimes it may seem like we are trapped when we endure the trials and test in the waiting, but God can and will bring us out. I remember hearing a song that had these words, "God will deliver on time". The pit is a low place, a place of darkness and dreariness. If we were to ask Joseph about the pit he could tell us he was once in the pit and God brought him out and put him in the palace.

Out the miry clay – Situations and circumstances can be messy. Miry clay is slippery, slimy and can cause one to sink. Trying to deal with our problems and to be placed on slimy, slippery clay is a double load. A lot of times we can't find our footing and with all we have to endure the load can cause us to slip and sink. Again God will bring us out. Scripture reads, *Ps 34:19 Many are the afflictions of the righteous: but the Lord delivereth him out of them all.*

Set my feet upon a rock – When we are given a something we can hold onto the burden is greatly lightened. When we think of a rock we think of it as being firm, solid and unmovable. When God gave Jesus He gave footing to the world. He is a sure foundation that will never fail and there we can stand. On Christ the solid rock we stand all other ground is sinking sand.

Established my goings - Many times when we are waiting on the Lord we need directions. Sometimes we can loose our way or just get lost in the cares of life. Usually we are constantly asking Him for instructions and to show us the way we ought to go. This lets us know that He will establish or confirm, direct or order our goings. *Goings* here means steps. In other words when we don't know the way he will give the direction we need.

Put a new song in my mouth, praises unto our God – Sometimes we sing sad songs or listen to sad music that depicts where or what we are going through. Not only that our complaining, grumbling and moaning can become our song. These things become our song and praise to God. Instead of singing a "somebody has done me wrong song" or just a plain old sad song, now we can sing Jehovah Jireh my provider you are more than enough for me. There should be a new song in our heart and a greater praise from our lips because of what He has done.

2. **Strengthens and builds character** - *Isaiah 40: 31 But they that wait upon the LORD shall renew their strength; they shall mount up with wings as eagles; they shall run, and not be weary; and they shall walk, and not faint.*

The qualifier for character building is waiting. Question is what is character? We hear that word a lot, and sometimes it is used loosely, but what is it? Webster defines it as the pattern of behavior or personality found in an individual or group; moral strength; self discipline. In layman terms simply put it is the basis for how we act daily. It's what makes us who we are. Looking at this passage of Scripture the writer gives us four promises that result in our waiting which will build our character. Let's take a look at them.

Renewed strength – This word *renew* in the Hebrew means to change, to alter; and then to revive, to renew, to cause to flourish again. This is what the Father wants to do for us if we will just let go and let Him. A lot of times we are trying to do things in our own strength which can wear us down emotionally, spiritually and physically. Emotionally our feelings can get in the way, and we may even act on them and totally mess up God's intentions for us. Our thinking is not in line with the Father. *Isaiah 55:8* reads, *"For my thoughts are not your thoughts, neither are your ways my ways, saith the Lord".*

We can become spiritually drained because we are doing all we know to do and don't see any results. Being emotionally and spiritually drained can lead to our physical strength being zapped. Thereby leaving us without energy to do the things we should and possibly doing things that we wouldn't ordinarily do. Anybody ever experienced just not wanting to get out of the bed after a challenging experience. What about being so tired that our bodies shut down letting us know that it's not going to do anything else; these should be signs for us to rest. It's only when we finally learn to rest, wait and expect the Lord to move in our circumstances that He can change, alter and then revive, renew and cause our strength to flourish again.

When our strength is renewed that means we will be given the ability to see and know the plots and plans of the enemy and know what to do to maintain the victory. We will be able to contend and make the right decisions and face the trials of life. It also means when we trust in God to deliver, we become strong in faith. Each time we advance to a new life experience our faith should be strengthened because of what happened the last time when God gave us renewed strength. We should become stronger and stronger each time a test or trial comes.

Mount up with wings as eagles – The word *mount* in this Scripture means to arise, or ascend up. Usually when we think of an eagle we think of how it soars through the sky high above the trees towards the sun. Not only is an eagle able to soar it is also a very strong and swift bird. For us that means we are to rise up or get up quickly from where we are stronger than ever. Mounting up with wings as eagles gives the ability to rise above our circumstances and situations because He has made us strong. We should be able to act or move quickly at any given moment. Finally, the more we soar above our situation the higher we should be soaring upwards to the Father.

Run and not be weary – *Run* in this passage means to move quickly. A lot of times when we are waiting we can't move as fast as we like, but when God steps in our strength is renewed. Not only can we run faster but we don't get tired. We will have a lot more pep in our step. Why, because now our faith as been confirmed our heart has been reenergized. Now we are able to make quick decisions.

Walk and not faint – These ties in with run and not be weary which basically carries the same meaning. Here we are able to get up and walk and not be tired. Meaning to move through the situation without falling out. God has given us strength to bear the trial without complaining and to continue on without being exhausted. *Gal 6:9 says, "And let us not be weary in well doing: for in due season we shall reap, if we faint not.* Don't get faint or allow our heart to fail when we are doing what we know to be virtuous, honest, true and of a good report. At God's own timing we will reap if we don't get exhausted or give up. If you are reading this book you should tell yourself right now **I can't give up now. I won't give up!**

3. God will deliver us - *Prov 20:22 Say not thou, I will recompense evil; but wait on the LORD, and shall save thee.*

There can be times when we are waiting on the Lord to answer us about an injustice that was done and this scripture can be a hard pill to swallow. Because we know we just want to go out and get somebody or just get even. However, the Bible says don't even say you will render evil must lest do it. *Say* means to commune, meaning to think or ponder in one's heart. We are not to even think, speak, utter or boast about repaying or rendering evil. The Word of God says to wait on the Lord, and He will save you. *Save* means God will do the liberating. He will give the victory, and He will be doing the delivering not us.

The following Scriptures help us to know that we are not to take matters in our own hands:
2 Thess 1:6 it reads "Seeing it is a righteous thing with God to recompense tribulation to them that trouble you;
Heb 10:30 "For we know him that hath said, Vengeance belongeth unto me, I will recompense, saith the Lord. And again, The Lord shall judge his people."
Rom 12:17 "Recompense to no man evil for evil. Provide things honest in the sight of all men".

Whoever has been foolish enough to do us wrong and know they did, the Scripture says God will *recompense* or repay those that cause us trouble. We don't have to do a thing, just wait on God to handle the matter.

4. **You will be exalted Ps 37:34** - *Wait on the Lord, and keep his way, and he shall exalt thee to inherit the land: when the wicked are cut off, thou shalt see it.*

I had mentioned this before in a previous chapter, and I think it's worth repeating. We may ask ourselves why is keeping His way so important? If nothing else comes to mind then it should be because it is commanded. The only other option we have is to do what's right in our own eyes, to take matters in our own hands and work our own agenda.

How many know that our way is generally not God's way. If God has not clearly given the way we should take and if a way comes to mind, and it's not according to His Word and His infinite wisdom, then it is self-will. **Self-will is sin.** What we need to do is to seek his face and make sure our heart is ready to obey once He's made known to us. Just as the Son did nothing in and of himself so it should be with us. Bottom line, again I say if we don't know what His way is then don't do anything. Wait on Him. Keeping

His way requires unquestionable obedience. The end of the matter is if we obey and do as He commands, we are rewarded.

This verse also tells us He shall exalt thee to inherit the land. *Exalt* meaning we will be raised up to inherit or possess the land. Question is what land? The land could be what every area in our life that we need to take possession of and have authority over. Think about it and ask yourself what is my land? The great thing about this is when the wicked are cut off or destroyed they will see what we inherit. There are people who are standing on the stand line waiting to see us fall. The wicked are the ones pointing their fingers and shaking their heads and making snide remarks, but God says I'm going to exalt you to inherit the land they are going to see it!

5. **Heart will be strengthened** - *Ps 27:14 Wait on the Lord: be of good courage, and he shall strengthen thine heart: wait, I say, on the Lord.*

After having to deal with folks and our own stuff sometimes it makes us want to throw in the towel and give up. This can cause waiting on the Lord to be a trying experience which can cause one to become fearful and discouraged. This Scripture reminds us to trust in the Lord; to rely upon Him; to come to Him in every situation.

While we are waiting it goes on to say to be of good courage, this means to be strong. Which goes back to what we were discussing early when the scripture said not to faint. This portion here has the same connotation that is, do not faint nor be dismayed. Continue to hope and trust in the Lord when all else fails.

He will strengthen thine heart goes hand in hand with Isaiah 40:31 as mentioned earlier. When we've given our all; that is our mind or intellect, our will and our emotions we need to be strengthened by the Lord. Our heart is the center or core of our will, intellect and feelings and after a while trials and test can take its toll on it. We become weak and that's when we need God's divine intervention. In strengthening us, He will able us to perform our duties, triumph over situations, circumstances and our enemies.

I believe David wanted to make sure that we understood how important it is to wait so he repeated it by saying, "Wait". Imagine how full David's heart was when God moved on his behalf; knowing that this waiting lesson resulted from his own experience. We all can learn from David and should fix deeply in our minds; that through hard times, difficulty, and times of danger, instead of sinking down in despair, instead of giving up, losing all hope and having a pity party, we should go forward and put our total trust in the Lord.

Prov 3:5-6 reads, "Trust in the Lord with all thine heart ; and lean not unto thine own understanding. In all thy ways acknowledge him, and he shall direct thy paths." As we mature in the Lord we will begin to understand how to give Him all our heart. As mentioned earlier, the heart is our core it affects our mind, our intellect, our will. It is the center of everything.

Postlude

Waiting…Final Word

As we have already learned waiting on the Lord can be one of the most devastating times in a person's life and then, on the other hand, it can be one of the most rewarding. It is totally up to us as individuals to decide which way it will go. I would say to you the reader choose the rewarding way. Earnestly seek God's face for clear direction that can only be found in His Word. Listen and obey that which He reveals and look forward to reaping the benefits.

Maybe this you and you are waiting for:
Ministry
 Job
Mate
Career Move
Baby
Love Ones to be saved
Home
New Car
Pay increase
Healing
Miracle

I know some will say, "Yes I can find myself on this list I'm still waiting and nothing has happened yet. What should I do? The answer is, wait.

Wait until the Father gives his instructions and seal of approval to move forward. Learn to really rest and find solace in knowing the Father will come through. No matter where we find ourselves in life know waiting will always be a part of our path. As I continue to learn to embrace this area of my life. I respect and acknowledge God's timing and realize when He's ready he'll do as He promises. Remember it's better to respond to a situation than to react. The Father knows what's best for you and for me
…..**Yet I Wait.**

Prayer:
Father, I realize I can do nothing in and of myself everything is dependent upon you. Even though it gets tough sometimes I'm going to wait on You. When it doesn't look like or I can't see anything happening, I'm still going to wait on You. When frustration and disappointment comes, I will wait. No matters what comes my way, I will wait. I know You know what's best for me. I will learn to obey and I will learn to rest. Thank you for your plan and purpose for my life. Thank you that after I have suffered a while you will make me perfect, establish, strengthen and settle me. Thank you for hearing me and being attentive to my every cry. Now Father, let your will be done on earth in my life as it is in heaven, in Jesus' name. Amen.